Remarkable Writers

Suzanne Collins

Megan Kopp

www.av2books.com

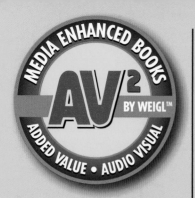

AV² provides enriched content that supplements and complements this book. Weigl's AV² books strive to create inspired learning and engage young minds in a total learning experience.

Your AV² Media Enhanced books come alive with...

Audio
Listen to sections of the book read aloud.

Key Words
Study vocabulary, and complete a matching word activity.

Video
Watch informative video clips.

Quizzes
Test your knowledge.

Embedded Weblinks
Gain additional information for research.

Slide Show
View images and captions, and prepare a presentation.

Try This!
Complete activities and hands-on experiments.

... and much, much more!

Go to **www.av2books.com**, and enter this book's unique code.

BOOK CODE

M 7 6 7 8 0 0

AV² by Weigl brings you media enhanced books that support active learning.

Published by AV² by Weigl
350 5th Avenue, 59th Floor
New York, NY 10118
USA
Website: www.weigl.com   www.av2books.com
Copyright ©2013 AV² by Weigl

Library of Congress Cataloging-in-Publication Data

Kopp, Megan.
 Suzanne Collins / Megan Kopp.
   p. cm. -- (Remarkable writers)
 Includes index.
 ISBN 978-1-61913-054-8 (hard cover : alk. paper) -- ISBN 978-1-61913-600-7 (soft cover : alk. paper) -- ISBN 978-1-61913-722-6 (ebook)
 1. Collins, Suzanne--Juvenile literature. 2. Authors, American--21st century--Biography--Juvenile literature. 3. Children's stories--Authorship--Juvenile literature. I. Title.
 PS3603.O4558Z73 2013
 813'.6--dc23
  [B]
                              2012003162

Printed in the United States of America in North Mankato, Minnesota
1 2 3 4 5 6 7 8 9 16 15 14 13 12

062012
WEP170512

Senior Editor: Heather Kissock
Designer: Terry Paulhus

Weigl acknowledges Getty Images as its primary photo supplier for this title.
Scholastic Inc/Scholastic Press: pages 5, 18 (Jacket art copyright ©2008 by Tim O'Brien); pages 5, 13, 19 (Jacket art copyright ©2009 by Tim O'Brien), pages 5, 13, 19 (Jacket art copyright ©2010 by Tim O'Brien); pages 12, 20 (Jacket art copyright ©2003 by Daniel Craig); page 21 (cover illustration copyright ©2006 by August Hall); page 13 (cover illustration copyright ©2007 by August Hall) Reprinted by permission.

Contents

Introducing Suzanne Collins

W ords have always been an important part of Suzanne Collins' life. As a child, she listened to her father's memories and stories of the Vietnam war and battle. She would also read and reread her favorite authors, soaking up their words like a sponge. When she was older, Suzanne read many scripts while preparing for roles as an actor onstage. She also wrote for children's television. Today, she is a best-selling fiction author. Her books explore the effects of war and the reality of violence. With the release of *The Hunger Games* movie, her words are being heard around the world.

Katniss Everdeen, portrayed by Jennifer Lawrence, is the central character in *The Hunger Games*.

Suzanne has won many awards for her books. Book **reviewers** have called her books original, imaginative, and enthralling. Suzanne has gone from an avid young reader to an author and screenwriter whose words have influenced readers of all ages.

 Suzanne and her husband attended the world premiere of *The Hunger Games* movie in Los Angeles, California. *The Hunger Games* was the number one film for four weeks in a row in the United States and earned more than $531 million worldwide in that time.

Writing A
Biography

Writers are often inspired to record the stories of people who lead interesting lives. The story of another person's life is known as a biography. A biography can tell the story of any person, from authors such as Suzanne Collins, to inventors, presidents, and sports stars.

When writing a biography, authors must first collect information about their subject. This information may come from a book about the person's life, a news article about one of his or her accomplishments, or a review of his or her work. Libraries and the internet will have much of this information. Most biographers will also interview their subjects. Personal accounts provide a great deal of information and a unique point of view. When some basic details about the person's life have been collected, it is time to begin writing a biography.

As you read about Suzanne Collins, you will be introduced to the important parts of a biography. Use these tips, and the examples provided, to learn how to write about an author or any other remarkable person.

Early Life

Suzanne Collins was born in 1962 in Hartford, Connecticut. Her parents were Jane and Michael Collins. Suzanne is the youngest of four children. She has two sisters, Kathy and Joanie, and a brother, Drew.

Suzanne's father was an officer in the United States Air Force. Michael Collins had a **doctorate** in political science and was a military **historian**. He taught military history at West Point Academy, a military school in New York. Suzanne remembers watching soldiers march on the training fields there. Suzanne's father also worked at other military postings, such as the Pentagon in Virginia and at the Air Command and Staff and Air War College in Alabama.

"I am fearful that today people see so many reality shows and dramas that when real news is on, its impact is completely lost on them."
– *Suzanne Collins*

The United States Military Academy at West Point trains cadets to become officers in the U.S. Army.

Each time Michael received a new post, the Collins family would have to move. In 1968, the family moved to Indiana. That same year, Suzanne's father was sent to fight in the war in Vietnam. Suzanne was six years old, and her father was gone for a year. When he returned to the United States, Michael told his family about his war experiences. He felt it was important that his children understood the stories behind battles, why they happened, and the consequences of fighting. Suzanne found these stories fascinating.

In fifth and sixth grade, Suzanne went to school in an **open classroom**. Open classrooms contain students of different grade levels who learn together. Her favorite subject was English. She remembers her English teacher reading stories by Edgar Allan Poe. Suzanne loved Poe's stories about the frightening and supernatural. She was also very interested in Greek **mythology** when she was young. *Myth and Enchantment Tales*, by Margaret Evans Price, was a favorite book. As she grew up, she read books by notable authors such as Kurt Vonnegut, George Orwell, and William Golding.

Along with his tales of horror, Edgar Allan Poe is often recognized as the inventor of the modern detective story.

Writing About Early Life

A person's early years have a strong influence on his or her future. Parents, teachers, and friends can have a large impact on how a person thinks, feels, and behaves. These effects are strong enough to last throughout childhood, and often a person's lifetime.

In order to write about a person's early life, biographers must find answers to the following questions.

1 Where and when was the person born?

2 What is known about the person's family and friends?

3 Did the person grow up in unusual circumstances?

Growing Up

When Suzanne was a teenager, the Air Force moved the Collins family overseas to Belgium. Suzanne went to an American school there from 7th to 10th grade. In Belgium, she learned to speak French. Suzanne also learned a little of the Flemish language, which is spoken in some parts of Belgium, France, and the Netherlands. Like many young people, Suzanne enjoyed physical activities such as gymnastics and running around in the woods with her friends. She also became enthusiastic about acting.

"I think the best thing to do if you want to be a writer when you're young is to read, just read everything you can get your hands on."
— *Suzanne Collins*

Get to Know Belgium

GREAT BRITAIN

London

English Channel

Amsterdam

NETHERLANDS

Brussels

BELGIUM

GERMANY

LUX.

Luxembourg

Paris

FRANCE

BELGIUM MAP LEGEND

Belgium
Capital City
State Borders
Land
Water

SCALE 0 — 125 Km   125 Miles

Later, Suzanne returned to the United States, where she attended Indiana University. She **majored** in theater and telecommunications. While at Indiana University, Suzanne met an actor named Cap Pryor. They later married and moved to New York. It was her goal to be an actor, but she later realized she wanted to do more than speak someone else's words onstage. She also wanted to write them. Suzanne decided to pursue a writing career and went on to earn a **master's degree** in dramatic writing from New York University.

Suzanne and her husband lived in New York City for 16 years, from 1987 to 2003. In that time, Suzanne switched from writing plays to writing for children's television programs. Eventually, she became a full-time book author.

📖 Indiana University is located in Bloomington, Indiana. It was founded in 1820.

Writing About
Growing Up

Some people know what they want to achieve in life from a very young age. Others do not decide until much later. In any case, it is important for biographers to discuss when and how their subjects make these decisions. Using the information they collect, biographers try to answer the following questions about their subjects' paths in life.

1 Who had the most influence on the person?

2 Did he or she receive assistance from others?

3 Did the person have a positive attitude?

Developing Skills

Earning a degree in dramatic writing helped Suzanne hone her skills and get a job as a writer. In 1991, Suzanne was offered a writing position at Nickelodeon, a children's television channel. She worked there for 18 years, writing for a number of television programs. Eventually, Suzanne became **head writer** on a television show called *Clifford's Puppy Days*. She also worked on another show called *Generation O!* about a young girl and her rock band.

"He kept saying you should write books, you should write books and I was like, yeah, yeah, whatever."
—*Suzanne Collins, speaking of her friend James Proimos*

The idea for Suzanne's first book, *Gregor the Overlander*, came after her friend, author James Proimos, encouraged her to try writing a children's book. Suzanne was walking through the streets of New York one day when her thoughts turned to Lewis Caroll's children's book *Alice in Wonderland*. Carroll's tale featured a girl named Alice who fell down a rabbit hole and into a strange, magical world. Suzanne thought that in New York, a person would be more likely to fall down a manhole than a rabbit hole. She wondered what Alice would find if she tumbled into a manhole. This gave her the idea for the character of Gregor, who falls through a laundry room drain in New York City and discovers the world of Underland.

Lewis Carroll's real name was Charles Dodgson. He wrote *Alice's Adventures in Wonderland* for the daughters of a friend. One of the girls was named Alice.

In Underland, there is a stone city populated by people and giant creatures such as rats, bats, cockroaches, and lizards. The book is about fantasy and war. Remembering her father's stories helped her to write the war scenes between the creatures in Underland. Suzanne also spent a great deal of time on the phone with her father discussing military strategy during the course of writing the book.

Every remarkable person has skills and traits that make him or her noteworthy. Some people have natural talent, while others practice diligently. For most, it is a combination of the two. One of the most important things that a biographer can do is to tell the story of how their subject developed his or her talents.

1 What was the person's education?

2 What was the person's first job or work experience?

3 What obstacles did the person overcome?

◢ The large buildings in New York City need many services, including water, electricity, and sanitation. Most of these services are supplied by underground facilities.

Timeline of Suzanne Collins

1962

Suzanne Collins is born in Hartford, Connecticut. She is the fourth child of Jane and Michael Collins.

2001

Suzanne co-writes an animated Christmas special called *Santa Baby!* based on the Christmas song of the same name. The special becomes very popular.

1993

Suzanne writes the episodes named "Blind Date" and "A Little Romance" for Nickelodeon's *Clarissa Explains It All* **series**.

2003

Suzanne moves to Connecticut. *Gregor the Overlander* is published and is selected as one of the New York Public Library's 100 Books for Reading and Sharing for 2003.

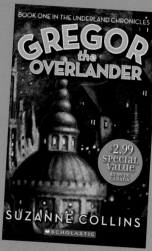

1997 to 1998

Working on *The Mystery Files of Shelby Woo* TV show, Suzanne writes "The Hit and Run Case," "The Alligator Mystery," "The Smoke Screen Case," "The Egg Mystery," and "The Spare Parts Mystery" episodes.

2005

Suzanne writes a children's picture book called *When Charlie McButton Lost Power*.

2009

Catching Fire is published. It continues The Hunger Games series, following the battles of Katniss and her companions.

2010

The final book in The Hunger Games **trilogy**, *Mockingjay*, is released. It becomes the number-one bestseller on book lists of *The New York Times*, the *Wall Street Journal*, *Publishers Weekly*, and *USA Today*.

Suzanne is also named one of *Time Magazine's* 100 Most Influential People in 2010. Others on the list include Barack Obama, Steve Jobs, and Lady Gaga.

2008

The Hunger Games is released for the young adult market. It is named a *New York Times* Notable Book and also wins several prestigious awards.

2012

The Hunger Games is released as a movie, starring Josh Hutcherson, Jennifer Lawrence, and Liam Hemsworth.

2007

The fifth and final book of Gregor's adventures in Underland, *Gregor and the Code of the Claw*, is published. It concludes the Underland Chronicles series.

Early Achievements

After completing the **manuscript** for *Gregor the Underlander*, Suzanne contacted Proimos' **literary agent**, Rosemary Stimola. Stimola specializes in finding new children's authors. When Suzanne described the idea behind *Gregor the Overlander*, Rosemary asked to see a sample chapter. She liked what she read, and the two women agreed to work together. Rosemary has helped Suzanne throughout the writing and publishing of all of the Underland Chronicles books.

It may seem there is a big difference between writing children's television shows and writing about war and survival. However, Suzanne's unique background helps her write about different subjects. She was already very skilled at writing for children, and her father's stories gave her a wealth of information to help her write about war.

Literary agents help authors get published so that their books can be sold in bookstores.

One night, while lying in bed, Suzanne was surfing the channels on TV. She came across reality shows that had contestants competing with one another for prizes. She also switched past channels showing news footage of war. She began to meld the two ideas together in her mind. The shows served as a source of inspiration for *The Hunger Games*.

📖 In *The Hunger Games*, a reality game show becomes a true battle between life and death.

Writing About

Early Achievements

No two people take the same path to success. Some people work very hard for a long time before achieving their goals. Others may take advantage of a fortunate turn of events. Biographers must make special note of the traits and qualities that allow their subjects to succeed.

1 What was the person's most important early success?

2 What process does the person use in his or her work?

3 Which of the person's traits were most helpful in his or her work?

Tricks of the Trade

Writing a story or a poem can be challenging, but it can also be very rewarding. Some writers have trouble coming up with ideas, while others have so many ideas that they do not know where to start. The writing process can be slow at times, but the results are worth it. Before starting to write, Suzanne learned that it is helpful to work out the structure of a story. She also thinks about what will fill the space in between plot points. As the story progresses, Suzanne allows her characters to develop.

Keep Your Eyes and Ears Open

Many writers get ideas by watching people and listening to conversations. If you pay attention, you will see that most people say and do all sorts of interesting things. These things can inspire writers to develop characters or to write funny or dramatic scenes. Like many writers, Suzanne uses experiences from her own life to create her characters. In both the Underland Chronicles and The Hunger Games trilogy, the main characters have lost their fathers. Suzanne used the sense of loss she felt when her father was away at war to develop her stories.

Write, Write, Write

Sometimes, the easiest way to finish a poem or a story is to write as much as possible in a first **draft**. This way, a writer can get all of his or her ideas down on paper. Then, the writer can decide which parts to keep. Very few writers have ever produced a great story in just one draft. Instead, they may review their first draft to see which parts should stay and what needs to be **revised**.

The Creative Process

Most writers have different opinions about when is the best time to write. Some work best late at night when everyone else is asleep. Others say that they are most productive early in the morning. There are also differing approaches to the writing process. Some writers need to make a detailed outline. This is a good idea for new writers as it will help them to organize their thoughts. Some writers do not use an outline. They simply begin writing and let their ideas flow. Suzanne approaches stories the same way, no matter what age she is writing for. First, she decides on the setting and the characters involved. As she writes, Suzanne keeps as close as she can to the personalities of her characters when facing the situations they experience.

It Takes Dedication

Writing takes dedication and discipline. Suzanne usually begins her day with a bowl of cereal and then sits down to work as soon as possible. If she gets too distracted before she starts, it is harder for her to focus on writing. By early afternoon, Suzanne is often finished for the day. She says that spending between three and five hours writing is a good day. Some days, Suzanne just gazes into space and works out character and plot problems in her head.

📖 Many successful writers begin writing as young children. Most had a love of words from a early age.

Remarkable Books

S uzanne writes stories full of meaning. Her books are often written for older children and teenagers, yet adults enjoy them as well. In both of her series, she brings together war, fantasy, and romance.

The Hunger Games

The United States as we know it has been replaced with the country of Panem. Around the controlling Capitol of Panem are twelve districts. The Capitol forces each district to send a boy and a girl to compete in the Hunger Games each year. The Hunger Games are a reality TV show, where the winner is the last person left alive. The winner becomes a hero and is given food for life. The book introduces 16-year-old Katniss Everdeen on the day of the lottery held to decide which two kids from each district will compete. When Katniss's younger sister is chosen, Katniss takes her place and begins the struggle of a lifetime.

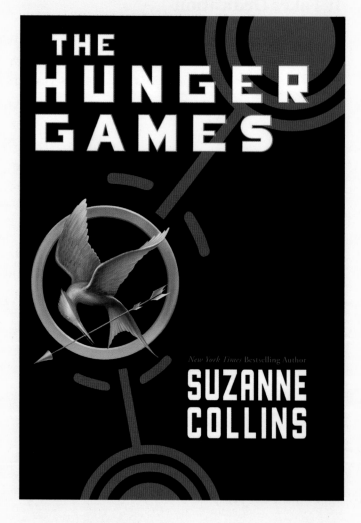

Catching Fire

After competing in the Hunger Games, Katniss returns to her family, but finds that feelings toward her have changed. There is unrest in her community. People in the districts are talking about rebelling against the Capitol and want Katniss and her friend Peeta to lead the rebellion. The 75th anniversary of the Hunger Games is coming, and something unusual is being planned to mark it. Katniss also must deal with romantic attention from two different boys. Brave Katniss has many decisions to make. *Catching Fire* ends with a big **cliffhanger**.

Mockingjay

Mockingjay is the last book in the Hunger Games trilogy. Katniss has become a leader of the rebellion against the Capitol. In *Mockingjay*, she takes the battle to the underground city of District 13. Together, the rebellion attempts to unite all the districts in overthrowing the Capitol. For Katniss, the battle becomes personal as she tries to save her mother and sister. In the end, she must choose between the love of her childhood friend or the love of her fellow competitor.

Gregor the Overlander

Gregor and his two-year-old sister Boots fall down a grate in their laundry room. They discover an underground world of giant cockroaches, bats, and much more. Gregor is desperate to get home. However, the humans living underground believe that Gregor is destined to help them. According to The Prophecy of Gray, an Overlander will come down from above to lead the Underlanders in their quest to defeat the rats. Gregor may be able to save Underland from destruction and find someone he lost long ago.

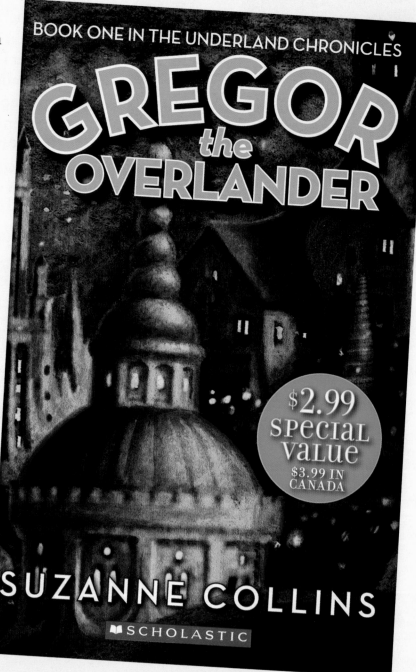

Gregor and the Marks of Secret

Life in the Underland has calmed down. Gregor finds himself spending more time with Luxa, the young queen. The mice that saved Luxa's life are disappearing, and she has vowed to find out why. They find a clue called the Mark of Secret. This frightening sign is an **omen** of death. Gregor and Luxa discover a horrible truth. The rats, led by the young and vicious Bane, want to get rid of the mice completely. Luxa vows to get revenge.

From Big Ideas to Books

Gregor the Overlander began with the idea of putting a big-city twist to the story of *Alice in Wonderland*. However, there was still much work to be done before it became a book worth reading.

Suzanne starts with a big idea for a book. The idea does not have much detail, just a basic outline of what will happen. When the outline is finished, Suzanne begins to research. Authors must learn plenty about their subjects so that their writing is accurate. For the Underland Chronicles, Suzanne read many books about bats, cockroaches, and rats. For the Hunger Games series, she learned about wilderness survival skills.

"One of the most memorable things I hear is when someone tells me that my books got a reluctant reader to read."
— *Suzanne Collins*

After researching, Suzanne sits down to write. Writing can be a long process. It took Suzanne about six months to finish the first draft of *Gregor the Overlander*. *The Hunger Games* was more difficult to write. The first draft took more than 10 months to complete.

The Publishing Process

Publishing companies receive hundreds of manuscripts from authors each year. Only a few manuscripts become books. Publishers must be sure that a manuscript will sell many copies. As a result, publishers reject most of the manuscripts they receive. Once a manuscript has been accepted, it goes through

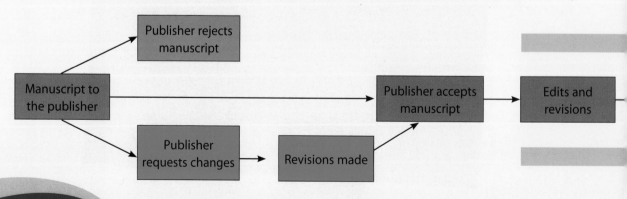

Once the manuscript is complete, Suzanne sends it to her editor, Kate Egan. Kate and a team of other editors read the draft and make suggestions for changes. The suggestions are sent back to Suzanne, who rewrites and improves sections of the book. The first *Gregor* book took a couple of months to revise.

After the draft is revised, the book is then copy edited. This stage of editing ensures that every sentence in the book is clear and easy to understand. **Copy editors** go over the spelling, grammar, and punctuation of the book and make everything read smoothly.

🖎 Most editors now review manuscripts on computers instead of on paper.

many stages before it is published. Often, authors change their work to follow an editor's suggestions. Once the book is published, some authors receive royalties. This is money based on book sales.

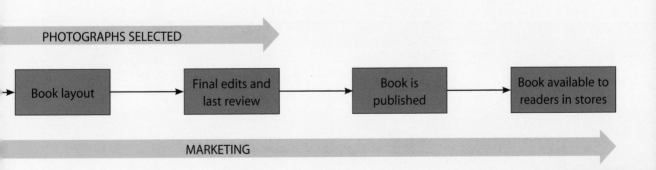

PHOTOGRAPHS SELECTED

| Book layout | → | Final edits and last review | → | Book is published | → | Book available to readers in stores |

MARKETING

Suzanne Collins Today

Today, Suzanne and her family live in the small town of Sandy Hook, Connecticut. The family now consists of Suzanne, her husband Cap, and their two children, Charlie and Isabel. Suzanne has not had much time to sit back and reflect on her achievements. When she is not writing, she makes appearances to promote her books. Her children often tease her about all the attention she receives.

Katniss Everdeen, as played by Jennifer Lawrence in the movie, uses her expert skills to survive during the Hunger Games.

Suzanne's biggest challenge has been her involvement in co-writing and consulting on the screenplays for The Hunger Games movies. Turning a 347-page book into a two-hour movie is not easy. The story has to be shortened to fit the time limit. The book is also written from a first-person **perspective**. This means that, in the book, readers are able to read about the thoughts of Katniss, the main character. The movie needs to be able to show events from Katniss's point of view, as well as that of other characters.

Gary Ross, who has directed films such as *Pleasantville* and *Seabiscuit*, was the director of *The Hunger Games*. The movie stars Jennifer Lawrence, who acted in *X-Men: First Class*, as Katniss. Josh Hutcherson plays Peeta Mellark, and Liam Hemsworth plays the role of Gale Hawthorne. The movie was released in March 2012.

Suzanne visited the movie set while *The Hunger Games* movie was being filmed.

Fan Information

Suzanne was not an instant success as a writer. Unlike authors such as J.K. Rowling or Stephanie Meyer, both of whom achieved fame with their first books, Suzanne's story is less dramatic. She spent many years writing for television before *Gregor the Overlander* became a success. However, it was not until the release of *The Hunger Games* that Suzanne became well known as an author.

Suzanne has always avoided the spotlight. She gives very few interviews and does not release very much personal information to the public. Unlike many other authors, her website, www.suzannecollinsbooks.com, does not have a **blog**, and it does not link to a Facebook page or a Twitter feed. Celebrity status is not something Suzanne really wants.

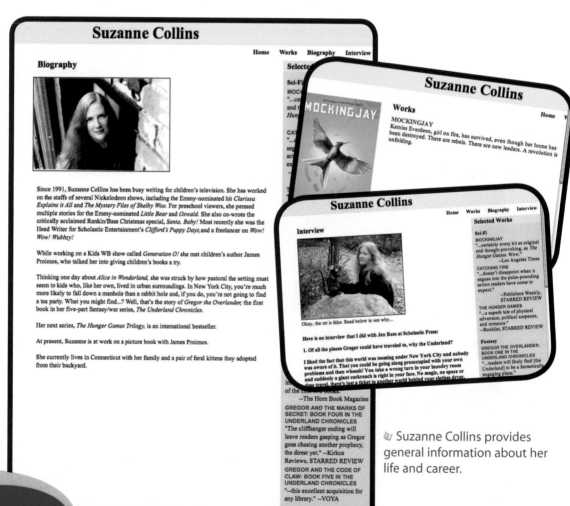

Suzanne Collins

Home   Works   Biography   Interview

Biography

Since 1991, Suzanne Collins has been busy writing for children's television. She has worked on the staffs of several Nickelodeon shows, including the Emmy-nominated hit *Clarissa Explains it All* and *The Mystery Files of Shelby Woo*. For preschool viewers, she penned multiple stories for the Emmy-nominated *Little Bear* and *Oswald*. She also co-wrote the critically acclaimed Rankin/Bass Christmas special, *Santa, Baby!* Most recently she was the Head Writer for Scholastic Entertainment's *Clifford's Puppy Days*, and a freelancer on *Wow! Wow! Wubbzy!*

While working on a Kids WB show called *Generation O!* she met children's author James Proimos, who talked her into giving children's books a try.

Thinking one day about *Alice in Wonderland*, she was struck by how pastoral the setting must seem to kids who, like her own, lived in urban surroundings. In New York City, you're much more likely to fall down a manhole than a rabbit hole and, if you do, you're not going to find a tea party. What you might find...? Well, that's the story of *Gregor the Overlander*, the first book in her five-part fantasy/war series, *The Underland Chronicles*.

Her next series, *The Hunger Games Trilogy*, is an international bestseller.

At present, Suzanne is at work on a picture book with James Proimos.

She currently lives in Connecticut with her family and a pair of feral kittens they adopted from their backyard.

Suzanne Collins

Works   Home

MOCKINGJAY
Katniss Everdeen, girl on fire, has survived, even though her home has been destroyed. There are rebels. There are new leaders. A revolution is unfolding.

Suzanne Collins

Home   Works   Biography   Interview

Interview

Okay, the rat is fake. Read below to see why...

Here is an interview that I did with Jen Rees at Scholastic Press:

1. Of all the places Gregor could have traveled to, why the Underland?

I liked the fact that this world was teeming under New York City and nobody was aware of it. That you could be going along preoccupied with your own problems and then whoosh! You take a wrong turn in your laundry room and suddenly a giant cockroach is right in your face. No magic, no space or time travel, there's just a ticket to another world behind your clothes dryer.

Selected Works

Sci-Fi
MOCKINGJAY
"...certainly every bit as original and thought provoking, as *The Hunger Games*. Wow."
—Los Angeles Times

CATCHING FIRE
"...doesn't disappoint when it segues into the pulse-pounding action readers have come to expect."
—Publishers Weekly, STARRED REVIEW

THE HUNGER GAMES
"...a superb tale of physical adventure, political suspense, and romance."
—Booklist, STARRED REVIEW

Fantasy
GREGOR THE OVERLANDER: BOOK ONE IN THE UNDERLAND CHRONICLES
"...readers will likely find [the Underland] to be a fantastically engaging place."

...of the first two books.
—The Horn Book Magazine
GREGOR AND THE MARKS OF SECRET: BOOK FOUR IN THE UNDERLAND CHRONICLES
"The cliffhanger ending will leave readers gasping as Gregor goes chasing another prophecy, the direst yet." --Kirkus Reviews, STARRED REVIEW
GREGOR AND THE CODE OF CLAW: BOOK FIVE IN THE UNDERLAND CHRONICLES
"--this excellent acquisition for any library." --VOYA

Suzanne Collins provides general information about her life and career.

It is difficult for Suzanne to avoid being famous, however. There are more than 16 million copies of all three books in The Hunger Games trilogy in print in the United States. *The Hunger Games* has spent more than 160 weeks in a row on *The New York Times* bestseller list since it was published in September of 2008.

In 2010, Suzanne did a book tour of more than 20 North American cities to promote the release of *Mockingjay*. Book tours may involve an author signing their books at stores and libraries, talking to fans, and speaking at schools. Since that book tour, Suzanne has been busy working on the Hunger Games films.

Suzanne's fans will be excited to know that The Hunger Games trilogy is being turned into four movies in total. *Mockingjay*, the final book in the series, will appear in the theaters in two parts. The popularity of the books and movie have led to the creation of Hunger Games merchandise such as collectible cards, games, clothing, and jewelry.

Fans could not wait for the release of the first movie. They flocked to theaters in droves to see it.

Write a Biography

All of the parts of a biography work together to tell the story of a person's life. Find out how these elements combine by writing a biography. Begin by choosing a person whose story fascinates you. You will have to research the person's life by using library books and the reliable websites. You can also email the person or write him or her a letter. The person might agree to answer your questions directly.

Use a concept web, such as the one below, to guide you in writing the biography. Answer each of the questions listed using the information you have gathered. Each heading on the concept web will form an important part of the person's story.

Parts of a Biography

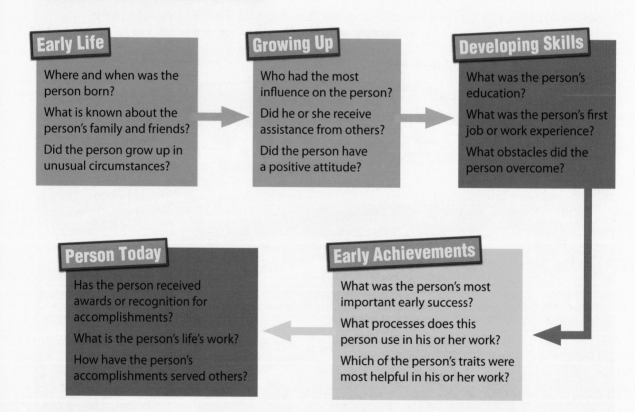

Early Life
Where and when was the person born?

What is known about the person's family and friends?

Did the person grow up in unusual circumstances?

Growing Up
Who had the most influence on the person?

Did he or she receive assistance from others?

Did the person have a positive attitude?

Developing Skills
What was the person's education?

What was the person's first job or work experience?

What obstacles did the person overcome?

Person Today
Has the person received awards or recognition for accomplishments?

What is the person's life's work?

How have the person's accomplishments served others?

Early Achievements
What was the person's most important early success?

What processes does this person use in his or her work?

Which of the person's traits were most helpful in his or her work?

Test Yourself

1 What was Suzanne's favorite subject in school?

2 According to Suzanne, what is the best thing you can do if you want to be a writer?

3 How long did it take Suzanne to complete the first draft of *Gregor the Overlander*?

4 What was the name of Suzanne's first picture book?

5 What did Suzanne do for 18 years before she wrote her first book?

6 What does Suzanne do after she lays out the basic storyline for one of her books?

7 Where does Suzanne live?

8 What is the name of the last book in the Hunger Games trilogy?

9 What does a copy editor do?

10 What was Suzanne doing when she thought of the idea for *The Hunger Games*?

ANSWERS

1. Her favorite subject was English. 2. She says you should read. 3. It took her 6 months to write the first draft. 4. Collins's first picture book was *When Charlie McButton Lost Power*. 5. She worked as a writer for children's television. 6. She researches her ideas. 7. Suzanne Collins lives in Sandy Hook, Connecticut. 8. The last book in the Hunger Games trilogy is *Mockingjay*. 9. A copy editor reviews spelling, grammar, and punctuation. 10. She was watching T.V.

Writing Terms

The field of writing has its own language. Understanding some of the more common writing terms will allow you to discuss your ideas about books.

action: the moving events of a work of fiction

antagonist: the person in the story who opposes the main character

autobiography: a history of a person's life written by that person

biography: a written account of another person's life

character: a person in a story, poem, or play

climax: the most exciting moment or turning point in a story

episode: a scene or short piece of action in a story

fiction: stories about characters and events that are not real

foreshadow: hinting at something that is going to happen later in the book

imagery: a written description of a thing or idea that brings an image to mind

narrator: the speaker of the story who relates the events

nonfiction: writing that deals with real people and events

novel: published writing of considerable length that portrays characters within a story

plot: the order of events in a work of fiction

protagonist: the leading character of a story; often a likable character

resolution: the end of the story, when the conflict is settled

scene: a single episode in a story

setting: the place and time in which a work of fiction occurs

theme: an idea that runs throughout a work of fiction

Key Words

blog: a journal written online, short for "web log"

cliffhanger: ending in suspense so that a reader or viewer is interested in the next story

copy editors: professionals who refine the spelling, grammar, and punctuation of a book

doctorate: the highest degree awarded by universities

draft: a rough copy of a story

head writer: the primary writer among a group of writers

historian: a person who writes about and studies history

literary agent: a person that helps to sell an author's work to publishers

majored: the main field of study

manuscript: a draft of a story before it is published

master's degree: an advanced university degree

mythology: a group of old stories that express the beliefs or history of a group of people

omen: an occurrence that is thought to be a sign foretelling an event

open classroom: classrooms with students of different grade levels who learn together

perspective: point of view

reviewers: people who assess books, plays, concerts, and shows

revised: made corrections, improved, or updated

series: a group of related things that come one after another, such as books that deal with one subject or character

trilogy: a group of three related works, such as books or films

Index

Log on to www.av2books.com

AV² by Weigl brings you media enhanced books that support active learning. Go to www.av2books.com, and enter the special code found on page 2 of this book. You will gain access to enriched and enhanced content that supplements and complements this book. Content includes video, audio, weblinks, quizzes, a slide show, and activities.

Audio
Listen to sections of the book read aloud.

Video
Watch informative video clips.

Embedded Weblinks
Gain additional information for research.

Try This!
Complete activities and hands-on experiments.

WHAT'S ONLINE?

Try This!	Embedded Weblinks	Video	**EXTRA FEATURES**
Complete an activity about your childhood.	Learn more about Suzanne Collins' life.	Watch a video about Suzanne Collins.	**Audio** Listen to sections of the book read aloud.
Try this timeline activity.	Learn more about Suzanne Collins' achievements.	Watch this interview with Suzanne Collins.	
See what you know about the publishing process.	Check out this site about Suzanne Collins.		**Key Words** Study vocabulary, and complete a matching word activity.
Test your knowledge of writing terms.			**Slide Show** View images and captions, and prepare a presentation.
Write a biography.			**Quizzes** Test your knowledge.

AV² was built to bridge the gap between print and digital. We encourage you to tell us what you like and what you want to see in the future.
Sign up to be an AV² Ambassador at www.av2books.com/ambassador.